Super

PREHISTORIC MAMMALS

Tamara Hartson

Contents

Geological Time Scale

The geological time scale is like a calendar of events in Earth's history. Different events cause the environment to change, causing plants and animals to change over time.

The time scale is divided up a bit like the way we divide schools. We have primary school, elementary school, middle school and high school. Each school is divided into grades and then classes. The geological time scale is divided into eons, eras, periods and epochs.

Eon	Era	Period	Epoch	
Phanerozoic	Cenozoic	Quaternary	Holocene	← 10,000 years ago
			Pleistocene	← 1.8 million years ago
		Tertiary	Pliocene	← 5.3 million years ago
			Miocene	← 23 million years ago
			Oligocene	← 33.9 million years ago
			Eocene	← 55.8 million years ago
			Paleocene	← 65.5 million years ago
	Mesozoic	Cretaceous	Late	
			Early	← 145.5 million years ago
		Jurassic	Late	
			Middle	
			Early	← 199.6 million years ago
		Triassic	Late	
			Middle	
			Early	← 252.2 million years ago

What are Prehistoric Mammals?

Prehistoric mammals are any mammals that were alive in the past, but are extinct now. Mammals that are alive today are related to these extinct species.

Many kinds of mammals existed in the past. Some were very large, while others were very small. Mammals even existed at the same time as dinosaurs! Both mammals and dinosaurs first appeared in the late Triassic period—about 205 million years ago.

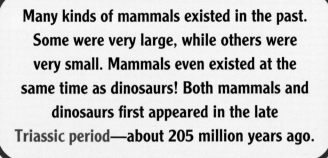

The images of prehistoric mammals you will see in this book are either drawings or computer-generated images. Sometimes they look like real photos. They can't be real photos, of course, because there were no cameras in prehistoric times! The images are estimates of what the animals and their habitat may have looked like based on fossils and where the fossils were found.

The First Mammals

The first mammals were small and looked a bit like modern-day shrews. They lived in burrows.

Modern mammals share these characteristics:
- they have hair or fur,
- most have live young instead of laying eggs,
- they produce milk for their young,
- they are warm-blooded and
- they have large brains.

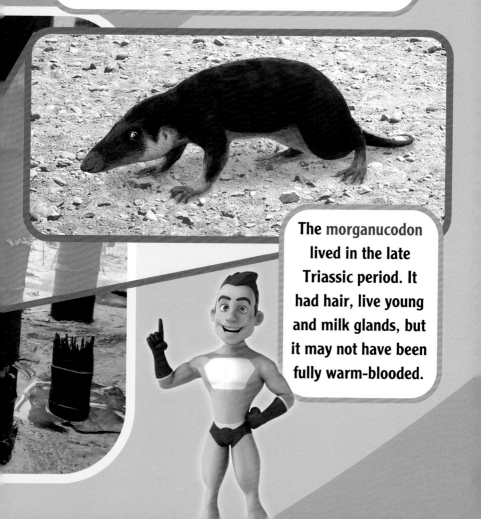

The morganucodon lived in the late Triassic period. It had hair, live young and milk glands, but it may not have been fully warm-blooded.

Alongside Dinosaurs

The dinosaurs ruled the Earth during the Jurassic and Cretaceous periods. Many mammals also thrived during these periods, but they were no bigger than a large house cat.

The mammals that lived during the time of dinosaurs ate mainly insects. A few, like the gobiconodon, were carnivorous, meaning they ate small animals, like reptiles and other mammals.

Gobiconodon

Dinosaur Extinction

The end of the Cretaceous period was 66 million years ago. A large asteroid hit the Earth and caused sudden and deadly changes.

The effects of the asteroid impact caused a mass extinction event. About 75 percent of all animal species died, including most of the dinosaurs.

Rise of Mammals

The deadly effects of the asteroid marked a new era called the Cenozoic. It is the current era in which we live. This era is also called the Age of Mammals.

In the Cenozoic era, mammals, birds and flowering plants began to thrive. The small mammals that lived alongside dinosaurs increased in size and kinds. Birds are the avian (bird-like) dinosaurs that survived the extinction event.

Glaciation

The Pleistocene epoch is part of the Cenozoic era. It began about 2.5 million years ago and ended nearly 12 thousand years ago. This epoch had at least 4 major Ice Ages, when glaciation took over much of the Earth. Glaciation happens when the Earth becomes colder, and the glaciers grow to cover much of the land. The continent of Africa was not glaciated, but it experienced extreme dryness.

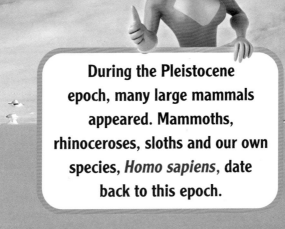

During the Pleistocene epoch, many large mammals appeared. Mammoths, rhinoceroses, sloths and our own species, *Homo sapiens*, date back to this epoch.

Megafauna

Unusually large animals are called megafauna. The Pleistocene megafauna evolved because of the cooler temperatures around the world. Large bodies are able to keep in more heat than small bodies.

Examples of megafauna are mammoths, rhinoceroses, giant sloths and cave bears. When the Earth warmed towards the end of the Pleistocene epoch, most large mammals became extinct.

Africa was less affected by the extinction event. That is why we still have elephants, rhinos and hippos.

Saber-toothed Cats

Saber-toothed cats are a large group of mammals that once lived all around the world. These predators had long front canine teeth that looked like fangs.

All sabre-toothed cats had a wide gape, meaning they could open their mouths really wide. They also had strong, heavy front legs.

The smilodon is often called a sabre-toothed tiger, but it is not a tiger at all. This strong cat was an excellent hunter. It preyed on bison, camels, horses and other large animals. Smilodon probably jumped onto its prey and held on with its strong front legs so it could bite its prey's neck.

The smilodon was one of the largest felids (cats) ever to exist.

Megantereon was about the size of a jaguar. Its front teeth were smaller than those of smilodon, but it was still a fearsome predator!

Barbourofelis is also called a false sabre-toothed cat. This predator looked like a cat, but it wasn't in the cat family at all! There are more than 130 known species of sabre-toothed predators, including cats and false cats.

Cave Lions

The **Eurasian cave lion** lived in what is now Europe, Alaska and Yukon. It is closely related to modern-day lions. This lion preyed on various kinds of mammals, including bear cubs!

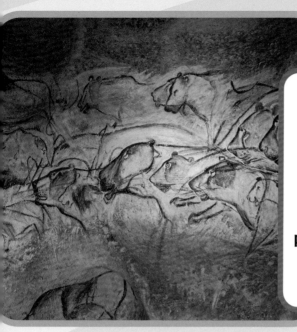

In France, cave paintings that are more than 30,000 years old show Eurasian cave lions chasing their prey. These lions went extinct about 13,000 years ago.

The American cave lion lived in North, Central and South America. Cave lions lived in cooler climates than modern lions. They made their homes in caves for warmth.

Bears

Cave bears lived in Europe until about
24,000 years ago. Their skeletons have been found
deep inside caves. Cave lion bones have
been found in the same caves as bears. The lions may
have tried to prey on the hibernating bears or their cubs.

The **giant short-faced bear** is the largest carnivorous mammal to have lived in the Americas. Males were larger than females. They were 10 feet (3 meters) tall when standing on their hind legs!

The **spectacled bear** that lives in South America is the closest living relative to short-faced bears.

Spectacled Bear

Dire Wolf

The dire wolf was a large predator that ranged over North and South America and Asia. It was a bit larger than wolves of today. Of all predatory mammals extinct or alive, the dire wolf had the most powerful bite!

Dire wolves lived in large packs. Packs can work together to take down larger prey than a single wolf can take alone. Dire wolves in North America mainly preyed on horses. They also preyed on bison, camels and mastodons. Dire wolves went extinct about 9000 years ago.

Hyaenodon

(hi-YEE-no-don)

Hyaenodons were carnivores that died out about 20 million years ago, and no living relatives are alive today. They preyed on many other mammals, even other carnivores!

The name hyaenodon means hyena-tooth, but they are not closely related to modern-day hyenas. They had enormous jaws that could easily crush prey and slice through skin and flesh.

Hyaenodons had large skulls, but they had tiny brains!

Woolly Mammoth

The woolly mammoth is one of the most well-known megafauna animals of the Pleistocene ice age. The last woolly mammoths lived on Wrangel Island north of Russia. They died out only 4000 years ago!

Woolly mammoths were covered in fur, making it easy for them to live in cold climates.

Males had much larger tusks than females. Tusks have yearly growth rings like tree trunks, so scientists can work out the age an animal was when it died.

The Columbian mammoth was closely related to the smaller woolly mammoth. It did not have as much fur, and it lived in warmer areas.

Columbian Mammoth

Mammoths, like modern-day elephants, were herbivores, meaning they ate plants. Adult Columbian mammoths ate more than 400 pounds (180 kg) of food each day! They weighed as much as five cars, and their tusks were as long as two bicycles!

Thousands of mammoth skeleton fossils have been found. The best remains are those found frozen in arctic ice. Several baby mammoths frozen in the ice have skin, hair and even food in their stomachs!

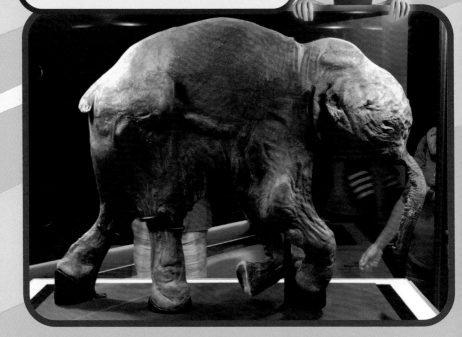

Modern-day Mammoths?

Scientists have been working to find DNA in frozen mammoths. DNA is the material that has all the information about how a creature looks and acts. If scientists can find perfect mammoth DNA, they may be able to revive the species. If it works, woolly mammoths could be walking in the Arctic again.
Do you think it is a good idea?

A frozen mammoth was found in Russia in 2012 by an 11-year-old boy!

Mastodons

Mastodons lived at the same time as mammoths, but they lived in a different habitat. Mammoths lived in open areas and mostly ate grass. Mastodons lived in forests and ate leaves, twigs and shrubs.

Mastodons lived in small family groups. Some young males may have lived alone.

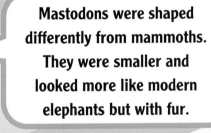

Mastodons were shaped differently from mammoths. They were smaller and looked more like modern elephants but with fur.

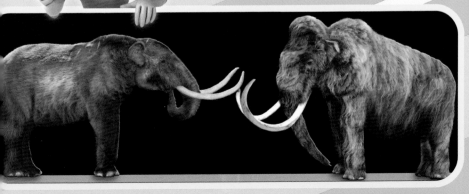

Stegotetrabelodon

(steg-ah-teh-tra-BELL-oh-don)

Stegotetrabelodon lived around 10 million years ago in Africa, Europe and Asia. It was bigger than a mammoth and looked more like an elephant with 4 tusks! Scientists think it lived in herds in forested areas.

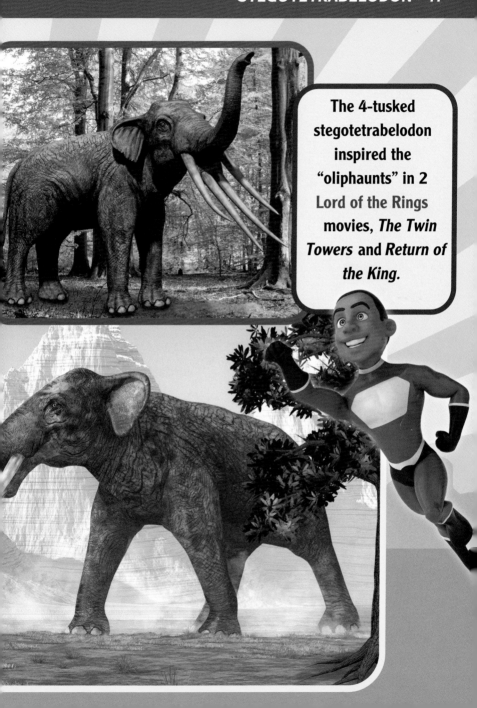

The 4-tusked stegotetrabelodon inspired the "oliphaunts" in 2 Lord of the Rings movies, *The Twin Towers* and *Return of the King.*

Deinotherium

(Day-no-THEER-ee-um)

Deinotherium was one of the largest members of the elephant family. Unlike most elephants, it could run for long distances.

The most unusual feature of deinotheriums was their tusks. The tusks grew from their lower jaw, curving down and backwards. They used their tusks to move and break tree branches so they could eat the leaves.

Platybelodon

(pla-teh-BELL-oh-don)

The gentle platybelodon was a small cousin to elephants. It was only a little taller than an average adult person and lived about 25 million years ago. Its mouth was shaped like a spork! That's a spoon and fork joined together.

Scientists first thought that platybelodons used their unusual mouths to scoop up plants from ponds and marshes. Now scientists think they used their bottom front teeth to scrape bark from trees. They used their small trunk to hold a branch steady while they scraped off the nutritious bark.

Arsinoitherium

(ar-sin-oy-THER-ee-um)

Arsinoitherium looked much like a modern-day rhinoceros. It was about the same size as a living white rhino but was actually related to elephants, manatees and hyraxes.

Arsinoitherium lived in and around ponds and marshes, and waded in shallow water to find plants to eat.

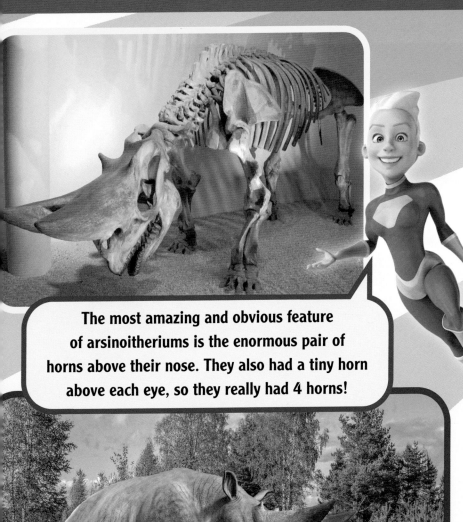

The most amazing and obvious feature of arsinoitheriums is the enormous pair of horns above their nose. They also had a tiny horn above each eye, so they really had 4 horns!

Woolly Rhinoceros

The majestic woolly rhinoceros lived during the Pleistocene ice ages in Europe and Asia. It had a heavy fur coat and could easily handle cold temperatures. It ate grasses and small shrubs.

These rhinos had one long horn and one short horn. The front horn could be as tall as a 12-year-old child!

Their images are easy to recognize in cave paintings made by prehistoric peoples.

Elasmotherium

(eh-lazz-mo-THER-ee-um)

The giant elasmotherium was larger than a woolly rhino and about as big as a mammoth. It is sometimes called the Siberian unicorn because it had a single horn. Like other rhinos, it was a herbivore.

Scientists are unsure if elasmotherium had a long horn or just a small horny bump on its head. Rhino horns are made of keratin (like fingernails and hair) and are rarely found as fossils.

Cave paintings in France show a rhino with a single horn that may have been an elasmotherium. If elasmotherium did have a horn, that would make it the largest horned rhino that ever lived.

Paraceratherium

(pair-ah-cer-ah-THER-ee-um)

The amazing paraceratherium was not just the largest member of the rhino family. It was the largest land mammal to have ever lived. The creature's skull alone would have barely fit in a bathtub! It didn't have a horn, but instead its nose may have been flexible, like a small trunk.

These large rhinos lived about 30 million years ago, long before the ice ages. They ranged over Europe and Asia, which was dry and desert-like at the time. They had to walk long distances to find leaves to eat in pockets of trees or shrubs.

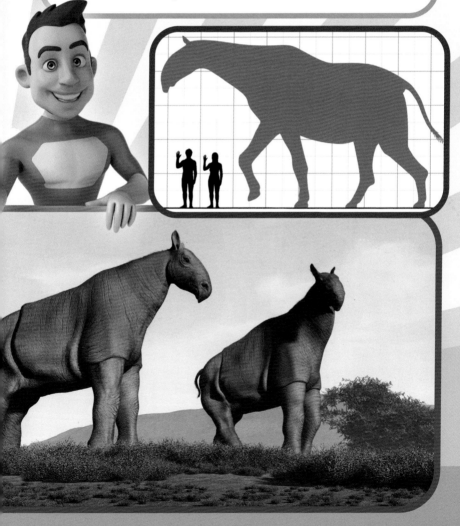

Giant Deer

The giant deer is also known as the Irish elk. It is the largest deer species to have lived. It lived in Europe and Asia in the Pleistocene epoch and went extinct about 8000 years ago.

Cave paintings in France show giant deer with their unique antlers. Their antlers were the largest of any deer species. From tip to tip, the antlers could be 12 feet wide (3 to 4 m) and weigh as much as 88 pounds (40 kg)! That's as much as a 12-year-old child weighs!

Kyptoceras

(kip-toe-SER-as)

Kyptoceras was the last animal of its kind. It was a small, deer-like animal with amazing headgear! Its antlers were not true antlers, but bony growths covered in skin like those on a modern-day giraffe.

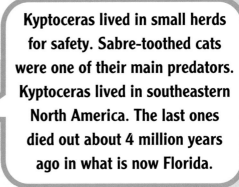

Kyptoceras lived in small herds for safety. Sabre-toothed cats were one of their main predators. Kyptoceras lived in southeastern North America. The last ones died out about 4 million years ago in what is now Florida.

Horses

In North America, the earliest known horse was called eohippus. It lived about 55 million years ago and is the ancestor of modern horses. Its name means dawn horse, or first horse, in Greek.

In Europe, one of the earliest horses was eurohippus. It resembled the eohippus. They were both about the size of a beagle.

Scott's horse looked more like a modern-day horse than earlier horses. It lived in North America until the end of the Pleistocene epoch. It was named after the paleontologist who discovered it.

Camelops

Camelops is a true camel that once lived in North America. It was closely related to the camels of Asia and Africa. It went extinct 11,000 years ago and was the last native camel to live in North America.

In Greek, camelops means camel-face. Scientists aren't sure if this mammal had a hump or not. They are pretty sure it had a face like those of modern-day camels!

Arabian Camel

Camelops had legs that were longer than today's camels. This may have been because they lived in shrubby areas rather than in the desert.

Antilocaprids

(an-TILL-oh-KA-prids)

The **tetrameryx** had 2 short horns and 2 long horns. It went extinct about 12,000 years ago.

Tetrameryx

Antilocaprids look like antelopes, but they are are more closely related to giraffes than to antelopes or deer! Several species of antilocaprids once roamed the prairies of North America. Today, only the **pronghorn** has survived.

Pronghorn

Stockoceros

Stockoceros was also a 4-horned antilocaprid that lived in North America, but its horns were much shorter. One of the people who discovered and described this species was a 14-year-old boy!

Giant Bison

The **giant bison** is the largest **bovid** to have ever lived. A bovid is a member of the bovine family, which includes bison, cattle, antelope and goats.

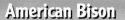
American Bison

This bison is called a giant for good reason. It was more than 8 feet tall (2.5 m) at the shoulder. From tip to tip, its horns were more than 7 feet (2 m) across! The American bison is still alive today, but it is much smaller.

American Bison   Giant Bison

Entelodonts

(en-TELL-o-donts)

Entelodonts looked like carnivores, but they were actually hoofed mammals related to today's hippos. They had canine teeth like a carnivore, but they were **omnivores**, meaning they ate both plants and animals.

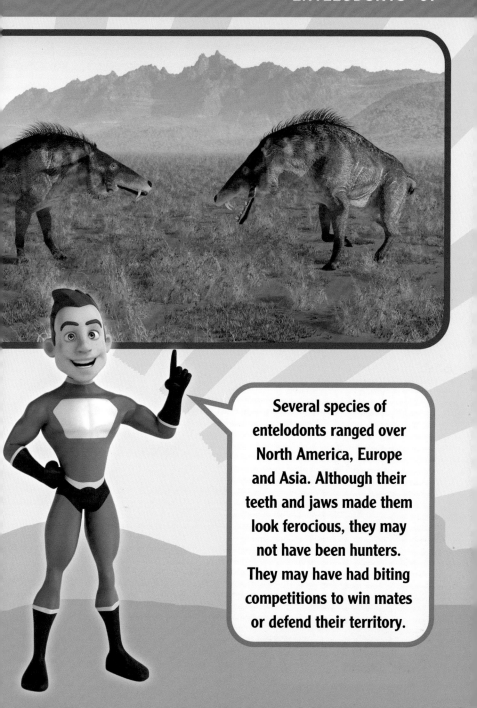

Several species of
entelodonts ranged over
North America, Europe
and Asia. Although their
teeth and jaws made them
look ferocious, they may
not have been hunters.
They may have had biting
competitions to win mates
or defend their territory.

Giant Sloth

The giant sloth was truly a giant! It was about the size of an elephant. This sloth lived in South America during the Pleistocene epoch. It had a large tail that it used for support while standing on its hind legs.

Giant sloths lived in grasslands and forested areas. They had teeth that were good for cutting vegetation. They ate leaves, grasses and shrubs. Like modern-day sloths, they rested a lot to help with their digestion.

Megalonyx

Megalonyx was smaller than the giant sloth. It lived in South and North America until about 11,000 years ago. Fossils have been found as far north as Alaska and Yukon!

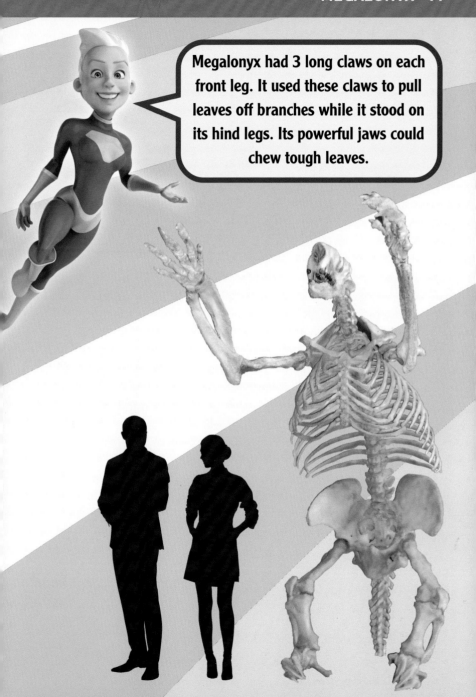

Megalonyx had 3 long claws on each front leg. It used these claws to pull leaves off branches while it stood on its hind legs. Its powerful jaws could chew tough leaves.

Doedicurus and Glyptodon

(dee-dih-KEW-rus)

Shaped much like a small car, doedicurus was the largest armadillo that ever lived. It had a long, clubbed tail with spikes that it could swing at predators. It may have also used its tail in combat when fighting for mates or territory. The top of its back was about 5 feet (1.5 m) high, and it was 12 feet (3.5 m) long!

Glyptodon was a large armadillo that lived in South and Central America. It was about the same size as doedicurus, but its tail was shorter and not spiked. Both glyptodon and doedicurus had a hard carapace for protection, much like a turtle's shell. They couldn't pull their heads inside their carapace, so they had a bony cap to protect their heads from predators.

Carapace

Thylacoleo

(thy-LAK-o-leo)

Thylacoleo is also called the marsupial lion. It is related to koalas and wombats. Unlike its plant-eating relatives, the thylacoleo was carnivorous. It had sharp teeth and a long claw on each front foot. It went extinct about 46,0000 years ago.

Based on its weight, thylacoleo had the most powerful bite of any mammal its size, living or extinct. It could easily take down much larger prey in less than a minute! Using its long front claw, it would hang onto its prey. Thylacoleo was not a good runner, so it probably had to surprise its prey.

Giant Short-faced Kangaroo

The giant short-faced kangaroo was the largest kangaroo to ever live. Like most other marsupials, it lived in Australia. It was nearly 9 feet (2.7 m) tall! Unlike living kangaroos, it couldn't hop but moved by walking instead.

This kangaroo had front paws with two extra long fingers with claws. It fed mainly on leaves, using its two long fingers to grab and bend tree branches.

Diprotodon

The diprotodon lived in Australia during the Pleistocene epoch. Like other marsupials, it had a pouch where its young, called joeys, grew. It had strong jaws for crushing the leaves and grasses that it ate.

Scientists believe that diprotodons lived in large herds that migrated to find food and water. These herds were mainly females with young and one male. Young males lived alone until they were big enough to win females and lead their own herd.

The diprotodon is the largest marsupial to have ever lived. The largest males were about the same height as an adult person.

Giant Beaver

The **giant beaver** lived in North America during the Pleistocene epoch. Like modern-day beavers, it lived near water such as lakes or rivers. Its tail was long and rounded.

American Beaver

The modern-day American beaver is much smaller than the giant beaver. It has a flat, paddle-like tail. The giant beaver ate leaves and bark from trees just like the American beaver.

Giant Beaver

American Beaver

Josephoartigasia

(ho-say-foe-ar-tig-a-SEE-ah)

The josephoartigasia is the largest rodent to have ever lived. It was even larger than the giant beaver! This creature was more than 8 feet (2.5) long and weighed over 1000 pounds (500 kg)! That's as much as an elephant weighs! It lived in South America in the forests along rivers.

Pacarana

The pacarana, a close relative of josephoartigasia, still lives in South America.

Capybara

The largest living rodent is the capybara. It also lives along rivers in South America. The capybara is less than half the size of josephoartigasia.

Ambulocetus

(am-byoo-low-SEE-tuhs)

About 48 million years ago, the ambulocetus was an early whale that had four legs. It couldn't walk well on land, so it mostly lived in the water.

Unlike modern-day whales, ambulocetus paddled with its legs to swim, much like an otter. It lived in shallow marine water and swampy areas.

Ambulocetus is called a transitional species because it links land mammals to whales.

Dorudon

(DOR-oo-don)

Looking a bit more like a whale than ambulocetus, dorudon still had four limbs. It had nostrils that were halfway up its head, like an early blowhole. The blowholes of modern whales are on top of their heads.

Nostrils

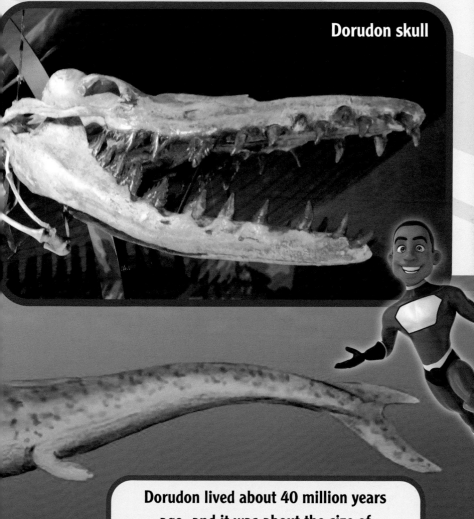

Dorudon skull

Dorudon lived about 40 million years ago, and it was about the size of a modern-day beluga whale. It still had tiny back limbs, called vestigial limbs. It was also one of the first whales to have tail flukes. Flukes are the flat parts of a whale's tail.

Icaronycteris

(ICK-ah-roe-NICK-teh-riss)

Icaronycteris is the earliest known bat. It lived about 52 million years ago. Scientists can tell from its ear bones that it could echolocate like bats do today. It also had backward-facing hind legs, meaning it hung upside down to rest.

Some animals use echolocation to locate food or find their way, especially in the dark. They make sounds and listen for an echo. Echos happen when sound bounces off an object or another creature.

Several complete icaronycteris fossils have been discovered in caves in North America. Scientists have found scales from moth wings preserved where the bat's stomach would have been! This shows they ate moths and other nighttime insects just like modern-day bats.

Purgatorius

(pur-ga-TOR-ee-us)

Purgatorius was a small, squirrel-like mammal that is the earliest known member of the primate family. It is the ancestor of monkeys, apes and even humans! It lived 66 million years ago, just after the dinosaurs went extinct.

The closest living relative to modern-day primates and purgatorius are treeshrews. Treeshrews live in trees. Even though purgatorius is extinct, treeshrews can help us understand the how purgatorius lived.

Treeshrew

Gigantopithecus

Although we have only fossil teeth and jaw remains of gigantopithecus, scientists can estimate its size. It may have been as much as 9 feet (2.7 m) tall when standing! This creature lived in the early and middle Pleistocene epoch in Asia.

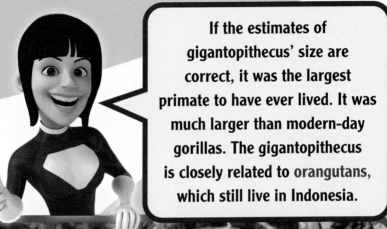

If the estimates of gigantopithecus' size are correct, it was the largest primate to have ever lived. It was much larger than modern-day gorillas. The gigantopithecus is closely related to orangutans, which still live in Indonesia.

Orangutan

Hominids

Australopithicus was an early ancestor of humans. These first human-like apes lived in Africa from 4.2 million years ago until they died out, about 1.2 million years ago. Australopithicus was about as tall as a 7-year-old child.

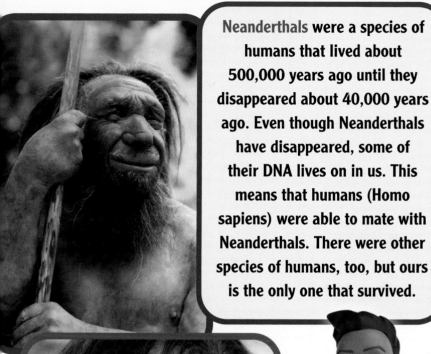

Neanderthals were a species of humans that lived about 500,000 years ago until they disappeared about 40,000 years ago. Even though Neanderthals have disappeared, some of their DNA lives on in us. This means that humans (Homo sapiens) were able to mate with Neanderthals. There were other species of humans, too, but ours is the only one that survived.

These images of hominids are photos of models at the Neanderthal Museum in Germany.

The Publisher: Super Explorers is an imprint of Blue Bike Books

Library and Archives Canada Cataloguing in Publication

Title: Prehistoric mammals / Tamara Hartson.
Names: Hartson, Tamara, 1974– author.
Identifiers: Canadiana 20230155448 | ISBN 9781989209424 (softcover)
Subjects: LCSH: Mammals, Fossil—Juvenile literature. | LCSH: Paleontology—Juvenile literature.
Classification: LCC QE881 .H37 2023 | DDC j569—dc23

Front cover: leonello/GettyImages

Back cover: Orla/GettyImages, Neanderthal-Museum, Mettmann/Wikimedia Commons, estt/GettyImages

Photo Credits: From Getty Images: al_la 61a; aphotostory (background) 43a; Aunt_Spray 28b, 33b; AVTG (background) 38, 41a; CoreyFord 18-19, (creature) 59b, 40-41, 42-43, 48, 51a, 57, 61b, 67; Daniel Eskridge 18a, 20-21, 28a, 49a; Dorling Kindersley (creature) 31a; dottedhippo (creature) 33a; equigini 63a; estt 53b, 68; hartmanc10 81a; Jillian Cooper 65a; kameshkova (background) 31a; KZhang (background) 59b; leonello 12-13, 17a; Musat 27c; Nouk 16-17; OlgaPtashko (background) 59a; Orla (background creatures) 10-11, 32-33; TatianaMironenko 83a; USO 93; vadimgouida (background) 33a; Warpaintcobra 27a, (creature) 41a, 43a, (creature) 45, (creature) 47b, 50, 52, 56, (creature) 59a, 66, (creature) 72, 89b; Xurzon (background) 44; Zoya_Avenirovna (background) 47b. From Wikimedia Commons: 3268zauber 91b; Adrian Michael 37; Andrew Savedra 89a; AnRo0002 (background) 77; Aram Dulyan 47a; Asier Larramendi 43; Bacon Cph 95b; Carlos Valenzuela (background) 91a; Charles R Knight 35a, 39a; Claude Valette 25a, 49b; Concavenator 92; Dantheman9758 (creature) 22, (creature) 38, 39b; DiBgd (foreground creature) 11; Films Oiseau de nuit (background) 62-63, (background) 64-65; Franco Atirador 55b; GFDL 27b; Ghedoghedo 8, (creature) 23a; Heinrich Harder 30, 42a; Jose manuel canete 74; Krzysztof Golik (background) 72; Marcus_Burkhardt 69; Matt Lavin (background) 76; Mauricio Antón 23b; MCDinosaurhunter 71; Michael B. H. 9; Neanderthal-Museum, Mettmann 94a, 94b, 95a; Nobu Tamura (creature) 44, (creature) 76, (creature) 77, (creature) 82, 84, 85, 86-87, (creature) 88, (creature) 91a; Patrick Lynch/Yale University 90; Pavel.Riha.CB 73; Roger_Witter 14-15; roman uchytel 46; Ruth Hartnup 36; Ryan Somma 31b; Sémhur 54; Sergiodlarosa 25b, 26a, 35b, 60; Steveoc 86 53a; Tylwyth Eldar 24; Woodtux (background) 62; Zátonyi Sándor 26b; ДиБгд 70; Создал сам 85; 先従隗始 87a. Other: National Park Service 6-7, 29, 34-35, (creatures) 62-63, (creatures) 65; Tamara Hartson 5, 83b.

Superhero Illustrations: julos/Thinkstock or Getty Images.

Produced with the assistance of the Government of Alberta. *Alberta* ∎
Government

We acknowledge the financial support of the Government of Canada.
Nous reconnaissons l'appui financier du gouvernement du Canada.

Funded by the Government of Canada
Financé par le gouvernement du Canada | Canadä

Printed in China

PC: 38-1